I LOVE ARABIC

Arabic Alphabet

Mohd. Harun Rashid

Mateen Ahmad

Arabic Translation

Prof. Tayyeb Abu Sin

ل

ذ

ك

ص

ق

GOODWORD

KIDS

First published 2014
© Goodword Books 2014
Illustrated by Gurmeet

Goodword Books
1, Nizamuddin West Market, New Delhi-110 013
Tel. +9111-4182-7083, Mob. +91-8588822672
email: info@goodwordbooks.com
www.goodwordbooks.com

Goodword Books, Chennai
82/324, Triplicane High Road, Chennai-600005
Tel. +9144-4352-4599
Mob. +91-9790853944, 9600105558

Islamic Vision Ltd.
434 Coventry Road, Small Heath
Birmingham B10 0UG, U.K.
Tel. 121-773-0137
Fax: 121-766-8577
e-mail: info@ipci-iv.co.uk
www.islamicvision.co.uk

IB Publisher Inc.
81 Bloomingdale Rd, Hicksville
NY 11801, USA
Tel. 516-933-1000
Fax: 516-933-1200
Toll Free: 1-888-560-3222
email: info@ibpublisher.com
www.ibpublisher.com

Printed in India

ث	ت	ب	ا
Thaa	Taa	Baa	Alif

ذ	د	خ	ح	ج
Dhaal	Daal	Khaa	Haa	Jeem

ص	ش	س	ز	ر
Swad	Sheen	Seen	Zaay	Raa

غ	ع	ظ	ط	ض
Ghayn	Ayn	Zwu	Twu	Dwad

ل	ك	ق	ف
Laam	Kaaf	Qaaf	Faa

ي	و	ه	ن	م
Yaa	Waaw	Haa	Noon	Meem

ا

Alif

Rabbit أَرْنَبٌ

لا تَسْتَطِيعُ الأَرَانِبُ مُقَاوَمَةَ الجَزَرِ

Rabbits cannot resist carrots.

ب

Baa

باص **Bus**

ذَلِكَ بَاص ذَا طَابِقَيْنِ

There goes a double-decker bus.

ت

Taa

Calendar تَقْوِيمٌ

يُبَيِّنُ لَنَا التَّقْوِيمُ الْيَوْمَ وَالتَّارِيخَ

A calendar tells us day and date.

ث

Thaa

Clothe ثَوبٌ

جَمِيعُ الثِّيَابِ الشَّتَوِيَّةِ دَافِئَةٌ

All winter clothes are warm.

ج

Jeem

Nut جَوْزٌ

تُحِبُّ السَّنَاجِبُ جَمْعَ الجَوْزِ

Squirrels like to collect nuts.

Haa

Ring حَلْقَةٌ

حَلْقَةُ الماسِ
A diamond ring.

Khaa

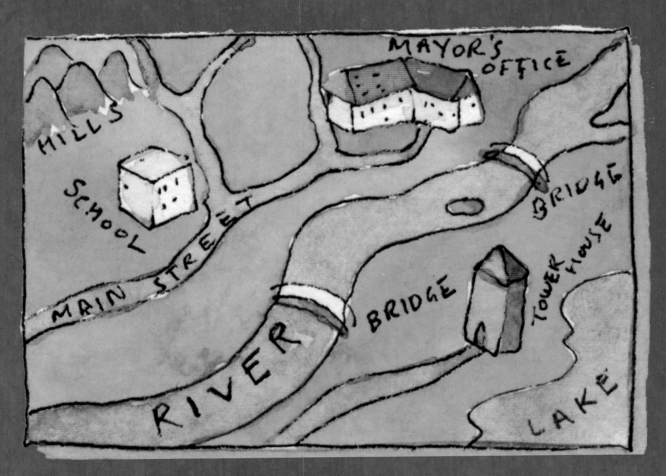

Map خَرِيطَةٌ

تُخْبِرُنا الْخَرِيطَةُ عَن الْأَمَاكِنِ

The map tells us about places.

Daal

Doll دُمْيَة

دُمْيَة جَمِيْلَة

A beautiful doll.

ذ
Dhaal

Tail   ذَيْلٌ

يَسْتَطِيعُ القِرْدُ التَّأَرْجُحَ مُسْتَخْدِمًا ذَيْلَهُ

The monkey can swing by his tail.

ر

Raa

Leg رِجْلٌ

لَدَيْنَا رِجْلاَنِ وَلَدَى الْحَيَوَانَاتِ أَرْبعُ

We have two legs; animals have four.

ز

Zaay

Giraffe زَرَافَةٌ

الزَّرَافَاتُ طَوِيلَةٌ جِدًّا

Giraffes are very tall.

س

Seen

سِنْجَابٌ Squirrel

تُحِبُّ السَّنَاجِبُ تَكْسِيرَ الْجَوْزِ

Squirrels love to crack nuts.

ش
Sheen

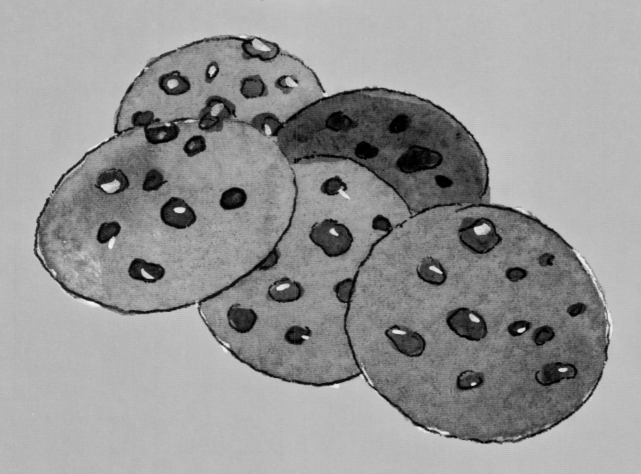

Chocolate   شُوكُولاَتَةٌ

نُحِبُّ كَعْكَ الشُوكُولاَتَةِ الْمُحَلَّى كَذلِك!

We love chocolate cookies too!

ص
Swad

Rocket   صَارُوخٌ

يَأْخُذُنَا الصَّارُوخُ إِلَى الفَضَاءِ

The rocket takes us into space.

ض
Dwad

Sheep ضَأْنٌ

خَلْفَ الضَّأْنِ أَسَدٌ كَبِيرٌ

A big lion behind the sheep.

ط

Twu

Aeroplane طَائِرَةٌ

طَائِرَةٌ سَعِيْدَةٌ

A happy aeroplane.

Zwu

Deer ظَبْيٌ

اَلظَّبْيُ حَيَوَانْ بَرِّيٌّ

Deer is a wild animal.

ع

Ayn

Spider عَنكَبُوتٌ

العَنكَبُوتُ الْمُرْعِبُ أَذْهَلَ سَامَ

The scary spider startled Sam.

غ
Ghayn

Cloud   غَيْمٌ

الغُيُومُ بَيْضَاءُ ورَقِيقَةٌ

The clouds are white and fluffy .

ف

Faa

Mouse فَأْرٌ

يُحِبُّ الفَأْرُ الجُبْنَ كَثِيرًا

The mouse loves cheese very much.

ق
Qaaf

Rainbow قَوْسُ قُزَح

قَوْسُ القُزَح لَهُ سَبْعَةُ أَلْوَانٍ

The rainbow has seven colours.

ك

Kaaf

Cake كَيْكَةٌ

إِنَّهَا كَيْكَةُ كَرَزٍ

It's a cherry cake.

ل

Laam

Toy لُعْبَةٌ

زَوْجٌ مِن اللُّعَبِ النَّاعِمَةِ الْمَحْبُوبَةِ

A couple of cuddly soft toys.

Meem

Clown   مُهَرِّجٌ

المُهَرِّجُ المِسْكينُ حَزِينٌ

The poor clown is sad.

ن
Noon

Fountain نَافُورَةٌ

النَّوَافِيرُ جَمِيلَةٌ

Fountains are beautiful.

Haa

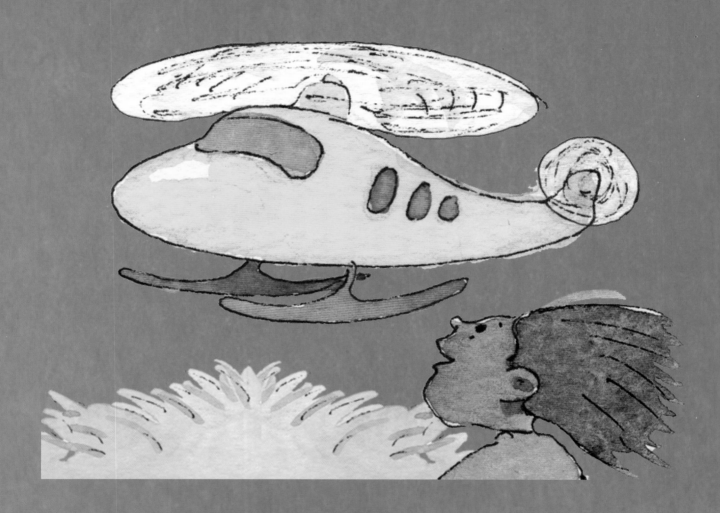

Helicopter هليكوبتر

أَرْيَاشُ هليكوبتر تُشْبِهُ الِمرْوَحَةَ

Helicopter rotors are like a fan.

و

Waaw

Pillow   وِسَادَةٌ

القِطَّةُ فِي سِنَةٍ عَلى وِسَادَةٍ

The cat is napping on a pillow.

ي

Yaa

Yacht يَخْتٌ

تُبْحِرُ القِطَّةُ عَلَى يَخْتٍ

The cat is sailing on a yacht.

Letter Fun
Circle the letters that begin the pictures

ق ب ث ي

ن ز د ذ

ش ك س ص

ف ن ق ث

س ص ش ك

م ز ق س